Tully and the Sad Day

Available in the Tales of Tully series

Tully's Life
This heart-warming story follows the journey of Tully from street dog to much-loved family pet, teaching young readers about the importance of kindness, understanding and hope.

Tully Takes Off!
Tully has arrived in her new home with her new grown-up, but she does not like it one bit! When Tully sees an opportunity to go back to her old life on the streets - the only life she has known up to now - she takes it with both paws. With a search underway, it is up to her new grown-up to work out what Tully needs and help get her safely home.

Tully and the Sad Day
Tully has woken up feeling grey and cloudy inside and she does not know what to do. She cannot help her big feeling because she does not know what it is. As her different feelings begin to work together in the wrong way, it is up to Tully's grown-up to help her to understand what she needs.

Go To Sleep Tully!
It is night time and Tully is tired, but she does not want to go to sleep. Her new grown-up knows that Tully is trying every trick she can to avoid going go to bed! With lots of adventures planned and Tully needing her rest, Tully's grown-up needs to find a way to help Tully learn to not be so worried about bedtime.

Tully and the Midnight Feast
Tully is a newly-adopted dog settling in with her new grown-up. Since her arrival, her snacks have started mysteriously disappearing from the cupboard and appearing under her bed, she seems to have forgotten her manners, and there are days when she just cannot stop eating! Tully and her grown-up need to work together to help Tully with her worries about food.

Tully and the Scary Day
Tully has woken up feeling scared. She isn't really sure why, but today feels like a very scary day, and she just wants to hide. Tully's grown-up is thankfully there to help Tully manage her big feelings and see that the day is not so scary after all.

Don't Touch Tully!
Tully is settling in with her new grown-up. She has learned that the new grown-up is a safe person and she enjoys strokes and cuddles with them. Then Tully starts to meet new people, who want to show her how loved she is. Unfortunately, Tully doesn't feel the same about people she does not know and trust. It is up to Tully's grown-up to find a way to help Tully with her big feelings and to be Tully's voice, when she can't use hers.

Tully and the Tummy Ache
Tully has a tummy ache and it's making her feel quite grumpy. She doesn't want to eat or drink, and she can't get comfortable. Her tummy is sore and it's getting worse! Tully is in a toilet muddle. So, Tully and her grown-up work together to sort the muddle out and help Tully to cure her tummy ache.

Tully's Birthday

It's Tully's birthday, and her grown-up has planned a special day for her, but Tully doesn't feel like celebrating. As the day begins to unfold, so do Tully's big feelings. Tully doesn't know what to do about the big feelings, so she does a bad thing. Luckily, Tully's grown-up is there to help her feel better about herself, and enjoy the rest of her birthday.

Listen, Tully!

Tully does not always like to listen, especially when her grown-up is trying to stop her having fun. Tully decides that instead of listening, she can be in charge. But when things start to go wrong, Tully and her grown-up need to work out how Tully can begin to find listening a little bit easier.

Tully and the Makeover

Tully has been having lots of fun playing in the mud, but now her grown-up says she has to have a bath. Oh dear! Tully is not sure she wants one of those. She is feeling a bit nervous about what is going to happen to her, but Tully's grown-up shows her that there is nothing to worry about. Having a bath is a good thing after all.

Tully and Vera

Tully has moved in with her new grown-up but she is missing her foster carer, Vera. Tully is struggling to understand why she had to leave, and whether it is okay to have big feelings about Vera. It is up to Tully's grown-up to try and help her to understand loss and endings and why, sometimes, they have to happen to make space for new beginnings.

Tully and the Chase

Tully loves to be chased. It gives her a feeling of excitement which starts off as being fun, but one day the excited feeling suddenly and very quickly becomes a feeling which is too big. Instead of feeling excited, Tully starts to feel scared. Tully and her grown-up need to work out how they can play Tully's exciting game without it becoming a bit too much for her, and causing a muddle.

Tully at Christmas

Things are starting to feel a bit different in Tully's house and all around outside. Tully's grown-up looks different, strange lights are appearing everywhere and people have started putting their gardens indoors! Tully is not sure what to make of this thing called Christmas – she just wants everything to stay the same. What can Tully's grown-up do to make Christmas-time a nicer time for both of them?

Tully Goes on Holiday

Tully has gone on a holiday with her grown-up. After a difficult start, things seem to be going well. But when the fairground opens up, with all its flashing lights, loud music and food smells, Tully's big feelings get the better of her, making her want to run. And she does! Tully's grown-up needs to find her in time to show her that holidays can be fun after all.

Tully and the New Rules

Tully likes lots of things about living in a house with her grown-up, but one thing she really doesn't like is all the rules! Tully thinks the rules are all very boring and her grown-up must want to stop her from having fun. One day Tully breaks her least favourite rule, and something bad happens. Tully doesn't know what to do! Can Tully's grown-up get to the bottom of this muddle so it doesn't happen again?

Tully and the Sad Day

TALES OF TULLY

Jess van der Hoech

Trauma Tools & Training

ISBN-13 978-1-83-81987-7-0
Editing by Sarah Ogden
www.jvtraumatools.co.uk

Acknowledgements

As always, to my trusted editor Sarah Ogden for all that you do to make these books come to life. I will never fully know what goes on behind the scenes, but it is a joy to work alongside you on these projects. Thank you.

To the children and families who I meet in my therapy room, from whom I have learned more about hope and healing than any course could ever teach me. Your input, ideas, questions and answers are so valuable to me and I will be forever grateful. Thank you.

Preface

There have been many occasions where I have been in my therapy room with children and teenagers, witnessing an expression of anger coming from them in varying degrees. Sometimes there is a huge rage, and at other times there is lower level passive-aggressive behaviour that is denied as being related to anger at all.

What I have learned over the years through observing this is that often, the feeling the child or young person has underneath the anger being displayed is more related to sadness, hurt, pain or fear. Displaying such feelings can be difficult – too vulnerable, too painful – and so these feelings are repressed, while 'anger' comes and steals the show.

For some children, not allowing sad feelings to come out can have manifested from an inadvertent encouragement from grown-ups to not allow them to be displayed. "Don't cry, I don't like it when you're sad, it makes me sad!" or suchlike comes from a place of love and kindness, but what does that then teach the child? That sadness is not okay? That sadness is an unwanted feeling, too difficult to be managed?

The same can be said when as adults we see tears, not just from children, but from any person. How many of us physically hand over a tissue to dry someone else's tears? What is the message there? Stop crying!

For children who have experienced early trauma, the act of crying may have earned different messages; that crying could lead to them being hurt in some way, or simply that when they cry, nobody comes.

When feelings are repressed, it is not unusual that they come back, albeit disguised as something else. And the easiest feeling to replace sadness is often anger.

Sad feelings should be honoured as much as happy ones. For the child who is stuck in their inability to display these feelings, Tully's story gives the opportunity to explore 'sad' in a safe way, allowing them to make sense of their own experience and feelings.

The Tales of Tully Series is based on the adoption of an ex street dog from Bosnia who came to live with me in September 2023. Watching her try to settle and adapt from everything she had previously known to fit in with a new way of life began to present a number of ideas as to how to communicate such difficulties that can be experienced, to others who are in the process of adopting or who have adopted children. The aim of the series is to provide an opportunity to explore different situations, circumstances, feelings and experiences, finding new ways of communicating and understanding each other, through the voice of Tully.

How to use this book

First and foremost, ensure that both you and the child are well-regulated and comfortable when you begin to read Tully's story. Make sure you choose a time when you are unlikely to be interrupted. The child may like a soother, a favourite or fidget toy, a drink or something to suck or chew to help them to stay regulated.

If the child is calm, then begins to try and distract or move away from the reading, make a note of what they have just heard in the text. It is very likely that they will have just provided you with some valuable information about something that they cannot tolerate or want to avoid for now.

The questions have been designed not only to explore the internal world of the child, but to help to develop a common language between the child and adult who are using this book together. The child cannot get the answers to the questions incorrect. Their interpretation of the thoughts and feelings Tully is having may provide some very significant information about the child's own thoughts and feelings. The child may want to expand the answers to talk about themselves and may even be able to make comparisons between Tully's feelings and their own.

Tully and the Sad Day

Tully had woken up with a very big feeling in her body. She felt it in her tummy and in her paws. She could even feel it in the tip of her tail.

Can you draw Tully and the big feeling?

Tully wanted the feeling to go away but she did not know how to make that happen. She was not even sure what the feeling was called.

What might Tully be doing while she is feeling like this?

Tully's grown-up walked into the kitchen where Tully was lying.

"Good morning Tully, it's a beautiful day!" her grown-up said.

Tully looked out of the window. It wasn't a beautiful day, it was grey and cloudy. Tully felt grey and cloudy inside.

What other words could be used to describe Tully's feelings?

Tully's grown-up stroked her chin.

"What's the matter Tully? You look sad," the grown-up said.

Maybe that's what the feeling was called. It felt heavy, grey and cloudy and Tully wanted it to go away.

What might Tully's grown-up have noticed about Tully that made her guess the feeling is 'sad'?

"Have a cry and let it all out," the grown-up said.

Tully could not possibly cry! When she was young, Tully had lived as a street dog in Bosnia. She had to take care of herself and her puppies. It was a hard job for Tully, but she had been good at it.

How might Tully have felt when she was a street dog in Bosnia?

Tully remembered when she was young there was a time when she had felt grey and cloudy inside and so she had a big cry. The noise had alerted some other bigger street dogs to where Tully was hiding and when they heard her, they came and chased her away. Being chased away had given Tully more big feelings.

What big feelings might Tully have felt after being chased away?

Another time, Tully had cried and a lady had come out of her house and shouted at her for making too much noise. Tully had started to think that her sad feelings were too much, so she had learned to switch them off.

What do you think of the plan Tully made to switch her sad feelings off?

When Tully remembered the big feelings she had when she was small, it made her feel a different feeling. The feeling made her growl and bark at her grown-up.

What might this feeling be?

Tully had switched the sad feelings off, but they were still inside her, making her feel sad and grey and cloudy. Sometimes, an angry feeling came to help so Tully did not have to feel the sad feeling.

Have you ever had feelings that helped each other?

Tully's grown-up sat beside her and stroked her head. The grown-up tickled her ears and scratched her chin. These were the things that Tully liked and made her feel safe with her grown-up.

What things make you feel safe?

"You are safe here with me," the grown-up said. "I can help you with your sad feelings. If you want to have a big cry, I will sit here beside you. You won't get in any trouble.

"You are never too much for me," the grown-up told her.

How might Tully be feeling now? What might Tully do next?

Tully thought about how it might feel if she let her big feelings out. She wondered if it would make her feel better.

What could be different if Tully let her feelings out?

What would happen next if she did not let her feelings out?

Tully started with a little whimper. Just a small noise at first. She felt her grown-up's hand resting gently on her back.

"I am here Tully. You are safe now."

Tully felt a big sob start to move around in her tummy. She did not want it to be there anymore. Tully let it all out, all at once!

"Awoooo! Ah....Ah....Awoooo!"

Can you draw Tully now?

When one sob came, another followed. Tully had the biggest cry she had ever had! Big tears and sobs left her body.

Her grown-up stayed with her and sat quietly as Tully cried.

When Tully finished crying, her grown-up stroked her and told her she was loved.

How might Tully be feeling now?

Tully and her grown-up sat together and Tully had a drink and a snack. Then her grown up took her for a walk and some fresh air.

Tully's body felt different, in a good way.

How might Tully's body feel different?

How else might Tully feel now?

Tully is learning that it is okay to have sad feelings. It is good to find ways of feeling the sad feelings and then letting them go. It is safe for Tully to have her sad feelings.

How else might Tully let her sad feelings go?

What do you do when the sad feelings come?

Who are your safe grown-ups who can help you with your sad feelings?

About the author

Jess van der Hoech is a qualified therapist who has spent the last ten years studying and working with the impact of developmental trauma and, in particular, the assessment and treatment of children and adolescents with complex trauma and dissociation.

As well as supporting birth families, Jess works with looked-after and adopted children and families, using skills in attachment-focused therapy and therapeutic parenting techniques.

Jess is a supervisor, trainer and motivational speaker with a passion for writing therapeutic books that are accessible to children and families to help with the healing process and to increase awareness in the impact of trauma.

Also by Jess van der Hoech

What A Muddle (2016) ISBN 978 18381987 0 1 (Co-authored with Renée Potgieter Marks)
An interactive, practical workbook designed to help children who have difficulties with emotional regulation to begin to understand what is happening in their bodies. A variety of activities throughout the book enable the child to start to explore these ideas through the story of Sam, while gently encouraging them to begin to verbalise their own experiences. Carrying out the physical exercises in the book can promote changes in emotional regulation. The text is written in a child-friendly, gender-neutral style, and is easy to understand for parents, carers and practitioners alike. For children aged 4-12.

These Three Words (2018) ISBN 978 18381987 5 6
Also available as an e-book. A unique therapeutic novel for teenagers with the aim of linking together the feelings, emotions and behaviours connected to anxiety, with some of the therapeutic tools that can be used in order to enable better self-regulation, increased confidence and different ways of thinking. The book is equally valuable to parents of teenagers with anxiety, giving them an insight and understanding into some of the issues that may be affecting their child, and potentially opening up a line of communication and a way forward between parent and teen.

These Three Words: The Journal (2019) ISBN 978 18381987 2 5
A thought-provoking and hands-on workbook, combining a series of practical exercises and tools designed to assist teenagers who are struggling with the symptoms of anxiety. Addressing the anxious responses in both brain and body, this journal provides the reader with the opportunity to discover therapeutic coping techniques and learn how to apply them to their own personal problem areas, before committing to a twenty-eight-day practice to promote good emotional regulation and reduced anxiety. The journal can be used alongside the therapeutic novel These Three Words, or as a standalone workbook, and it is suitable for use by the teenage reader on their own, with a parent, or in a group.

Beastie, Baby and the Brand-New Mummy (2022) ISBN 978 18381987 3 2 and *Beastie, Baby and the Brand-New Daddy (2022) ISBN 978 18381987 4 9*
A therapeutic story that looks at the external signs of pathological dissociation in a child. Dolly's story helps children who have experienced early trauma to begin to understand, in a very simple way, what dissociation is and why it has happened in their internal world. Tools and techniques are included within the story that parents and caregivers can use to assist the child in the first stages of their healing process. Beautiful illustrations on every page enhance the story of Dolly, and help the reader to relate to the events that happen, to notice the methods Dolly has developed to manage her feelings, and to think about what is happening in their own internal world. For children aged 4-12

Printed in Great Britain
by Amazon